SIGN LANGUAGE SERIES

Family and Community

Designed and Illustrated by
Jane Schneider and Kathy Kifer

Published by

Garlic Press
605 Powers Street
Eugene, OR 97402

www.garlicpress.com

ISBN 0-931993-73-3

Family and Community

Come, view our Family Album. Meet our neighbors. And meet those who work in our Community.

The people, pictures, and signs to follow have been chosen to show the relationships which structure the Family and the Community for which beginning signers should gain a familiarity.

As much as possible, we have chosen to present the most universal signs, knowing that there may be other variations.

Minister

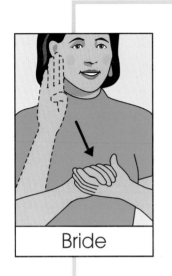

Bride

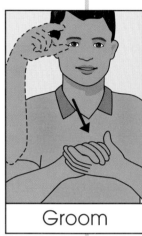

Groom

Mrs.

Mr.

Miss/Ms.

Occupations and Gender

Family & Community presents family members and relationships as well as community members in their job roles. The common signs and accompanying pictures should prove popular to young signers.

Here are two helpful points about signing. First, signs that indicate gender have common positions. Many female-related signs are positioned near the cheek, mouth, or chin area. Many male-related signs are positioned from the forehead to the head area.

These positions are demonstrated on the opposite page with bride, Mrs., and Miss/Ms. for female signs and groom and Mr. for male signs. Watch for these distinctions in the **Family Album** to follow.

Second, in the **Community Section**, occupations usually have a common sign (person) that is combined with another sign to distinguish a particular occupation. For instance, the sign for fire combines with person to give fire fighter (fire person); the police sign combines with person to give police officer (police person); or, the sign for cook combines with the person sign to give chef (cook person).

Bricklayer *(brick person)*

Family

Father

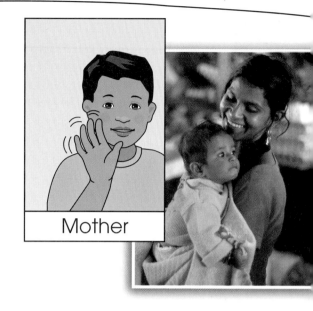

Mother

Daughter

Son

Sister

Brother

Baby

Twins

Uncle

Aunt

Niece

Nephew

Cousin

Grandma

Grandpa

Grandparent

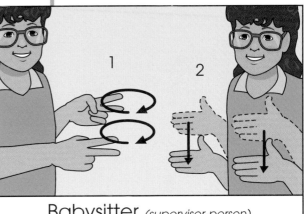

Babysitter *(supervisor-person)*

Neighborhood

Friend   Guest

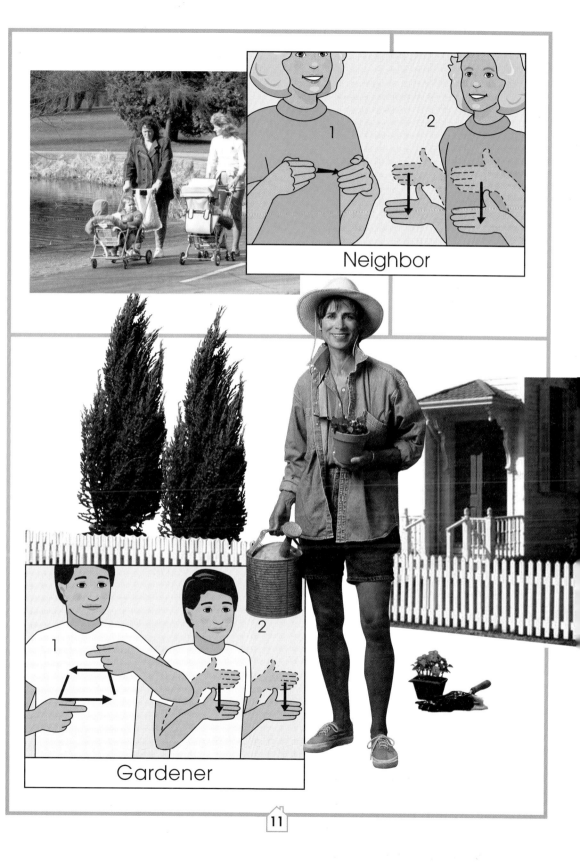

Neighbor

Gardener

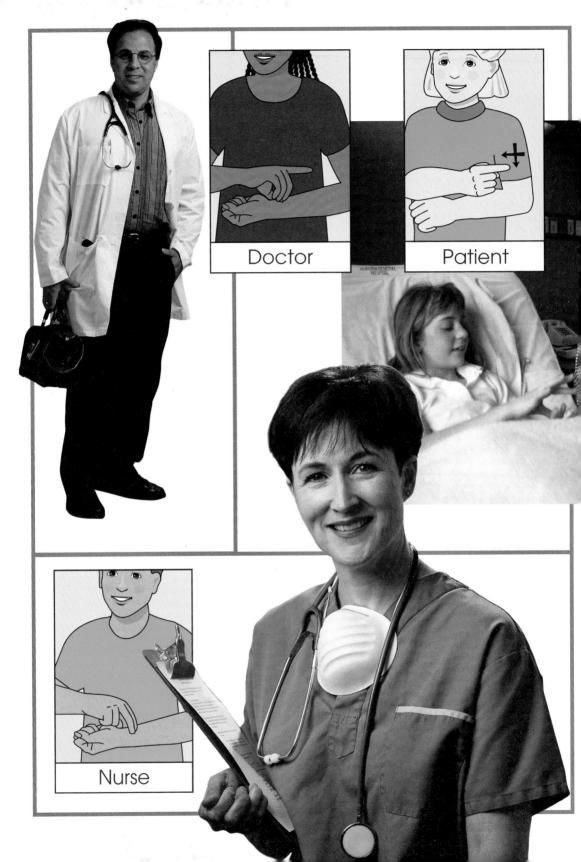

Doctor

Patient

Nurse

Emergency Workers

Fire Fighter

Police Officer

School

Teacher

Graduate

Music Teacher

Principal

Student *(learn-person)*

P-E Teacher

15

Sports

Soccer

Basketball

Bicycling

Ice Skating

Baseball

Running

Football

Florist *(flower person)*

Grocery Clerk *(food person)*

Hair Stylist *(cut-person)*

Seamstress *(sew-person)*

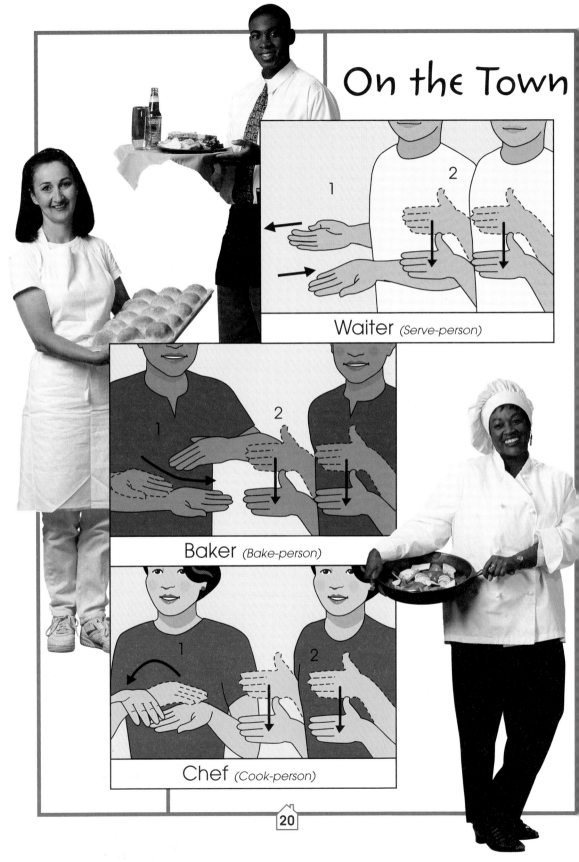

Waiter *(Serve-person)*

Baker *(Bake-person)*

Chef *(Cook-person)*

Singer

Musician *(music-person)*

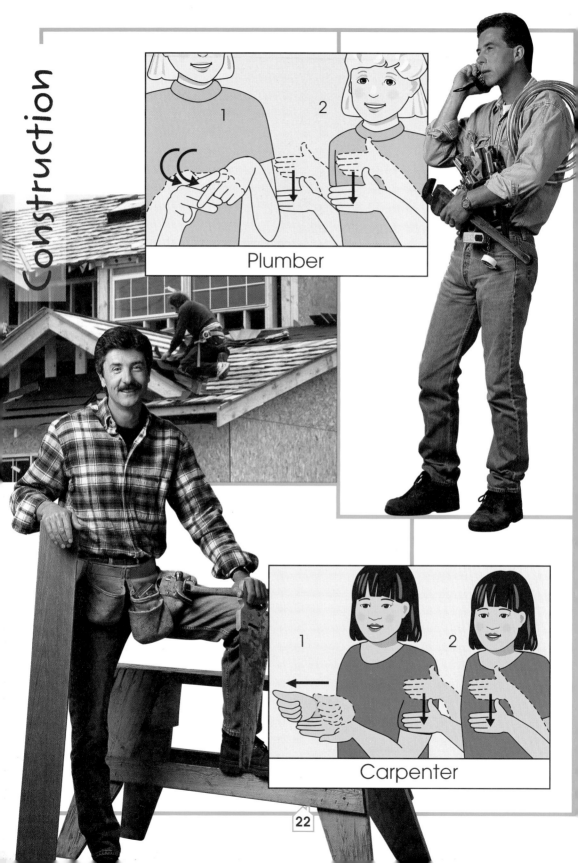

Plumber

Carpenter

Architect

Electrician *(electric-person)*

News and Legal

Lawyer

Judge *(decision-person)*

Librarian

Editor *(correct-person)*

Photographer

Reporter

Other Occupations

Artist

Computer Worker

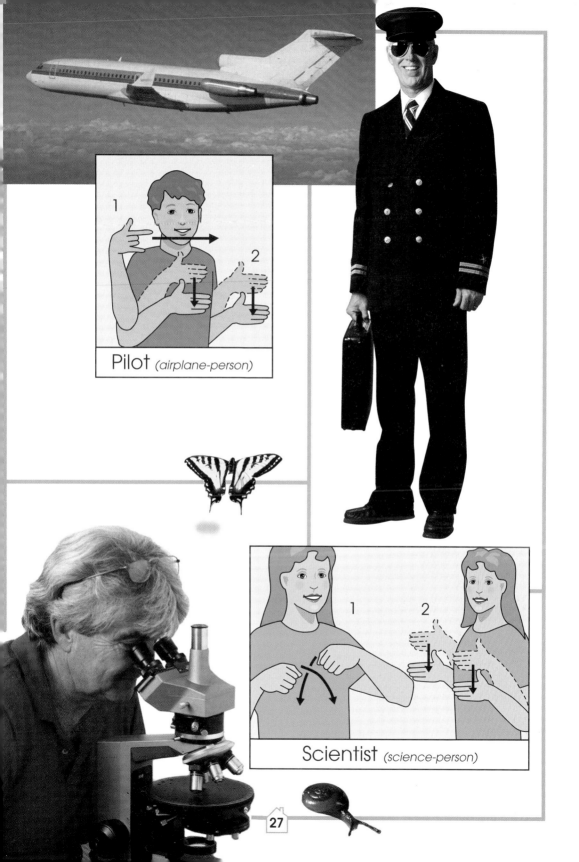

Pilot *(airplane-person)*

Scientist *(science-person)*

Delivery Person

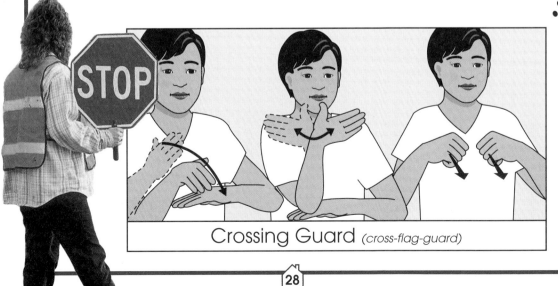

Crossing Guard (cross-flag-guard)

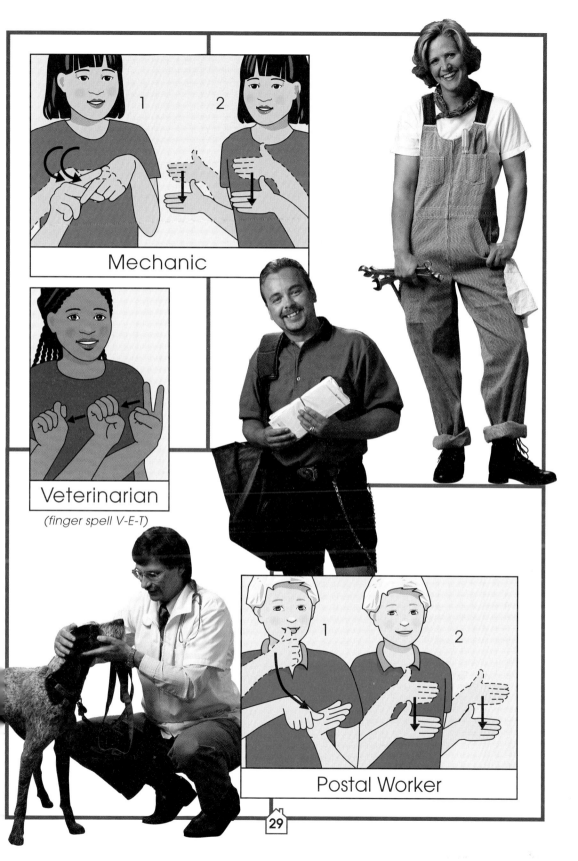

Mechanic

Veterinarian

(finger spell V-E-T)

Postal Worker

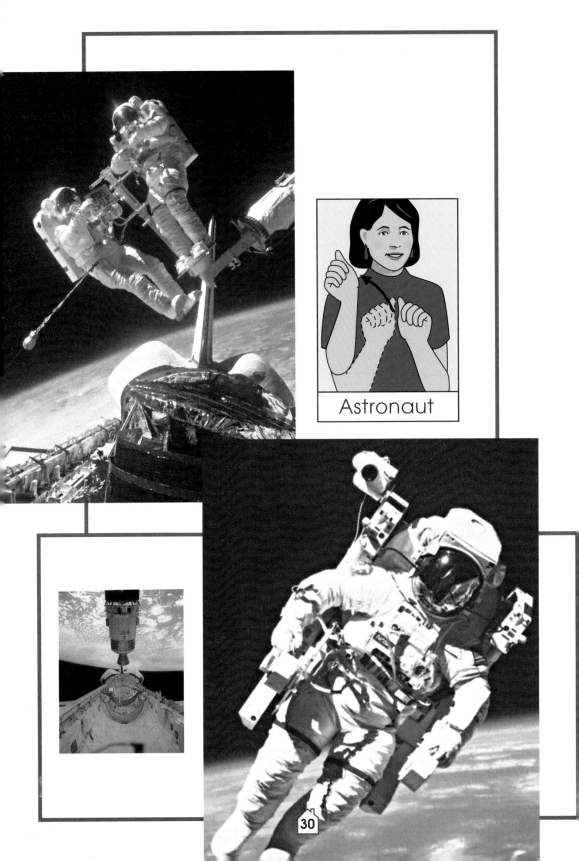

Astronaut

Index

Also from Garlic Press

Finger Alphabet GP-046
Uses word games and activities to teach the finger alphabet.

Signing in School GP-047
Presents signs needed in a school setting.

Can I Help? Helping the Hearing Impaired in Emergency Situations
GP-057 Signs, sentences and information to help communicate with the hearing impaired.

Caring for Young Children: Signing for Day Care Providers and Sitters
GP-058 Signs for feelings, directions, activities and foods, bedtime, discipline and comfort-giving.

An Alphabet of Animal Signs
GP-065 Animal illustrations and associated signs for each letter of the alphabet.

Mother Goose in Sign
GP-066 Fully illustrated nursery rhymes.

Number and Letter Games
GP-072 Presents a variety of games involving the finger alphabet and sign numbers.

Expanded Songs in Sign
GP-005 Eleven songs in Signed English. The easy-to-follow illustrations enable you to sign along.

Foods GP-087
A colorful collection of photos with signs for 43 common foods.

Fruits & Vegetables GP-088
Thirty-nine beautiful photos with signs.

Pets, Animals & Creatures
GP-089 Seventy-seven photos with signs of pets, animals & creatures familiar to signers of all ages.

Signing at Church
GP-098 For adults and young adults. Helpful phrases, the Lord's Prayer and *John 3:16*.

Signing at Sunday School
GP-099 Phrases, songs, Bible verses and the story of Jesus clearly illustrated.

Coyote & Bobcat
GP-081 A Navajo story serving to tell how Coyote and Bobcat got their shapes.

Raven & Water Monster
GP-082 This Haida story tells how Raven gained his beautiful black color and how he brought water to the earth.

Fountain of Youth
GP-086 This Korean folk tale about neighbors shows the rewards of kindness and the folly of greed.

Ananse the Spider: Why Spiders Stay on the Ceiling
GP-085 A West African folk tale about the boastful spider Ananse and why he now hides in dark corners.

www.garlicpress.com